ANT OR SLOTH:

Which will you be?

by

Steve Kelly

TABLE OF CONTENTS

INTRODUCTION

It's natural to desire significance, or even prominence in life. Everyone wants to be somebody. We were born with gifts and purpose and an innate desire to achieve. God's desire is that we fulfill our desires, so long as they align with His. In fact, He says that if we "take delight in the Lord, He will give you the desires of your heart."[1]

So, if everybody wants to be somebody, and God will give us the desires of our heart, why are so many people unfulfilled in this life? Why are so many people failing to achieve their potential? What is the secret to success? Why does it seem that only a few people are able to achieve great things?

The answer is found in the title of this book, and it's found in your choice to mirror either the ant or the sloth with your life. The secret to success is no secret at all. It's been around since the beginning of time, and it remains available to anyone who is willing to work. The development of your destiny comes down to one simple word: Leadership.

All the ambition and desire and dreaming in the world is rendered ineffective if there is no leadership in action to make ideas reality. Take leadership over your decisions and you will see the manifestation of those ambitions, if you are patient and faithful. Once you take leadership over your own actions and decisions, you will be given more opportunity to lead. You will be given the opportunity to flourish and grow and leave a legacy for the generations to come.

There's no doubt God expects us to lead ourselves before we can lead others in any supervisory role. Whether it's in family, business or community. It's the little things that matter, like balancing your checkbook or being on time for appointments.

In this book, we're going to look at the ant and the sloth as examples for how we should live (and not live). We're going to learn some things about ourselves based on how the ant and the sloth live. If you're open to it, we will probably uncover some slothful habits that can be removed from your life. If you're open to it, we will find some examples from the ant that might be hard, but will lead to victory and achievement in your life.

Before we get started, let me remind you that this isn't going to be easy. Obviously, living like the sloth is the wrong way to go. Living like the ant is the productive, fulfilling course to take. If you're looking for a shortcut you might as well put this book down now. If you were hoping there was a secret formula or magic recipe for success, sorry; it doesn't exist. The ant works hard. The sloth hardly works. If you're ready to work hard and achieve great things for God and your family, then read on.

Proverbs 6:6-8 (NIV) is a frequently quoted Scripture about the importance of hard work. If you've been a Christian (or even if not) for any length of time, it's pretty likely you've heard these verses mentioned at least once:

"Go to the ant, you sluggard; consider its ways and be wise: it has no commander, overseer or ruler, yet it stores its provisions in summer and gathers its food at harvest."

In this brief passage, Solomon points out an example for all people, found in the life and work of the tiny ant. This small bug, as common as dirt, is highlighted by God as an inspiration for how we should live. Some might think that it's strange, but God always uses the insignificant to teach us about what really matters in life.

Over the course of my own life and ministry, I've experienced seasons of productivity where I lived like the ant. I was diligent and prudent and worked hard. The result of that diligence was a harvest. Just like the ant, I was preparing for my future by the work I did every day. My hope is that everyone chooses to follow the example of the ant.

There is another creature mentioned many times in the book of Proverbs. Interestingly, it's not the actual creature that is spotlighted; it's a characteristic. That animal is the sloth. The characteristic is his sluggishness. The sloth or sluggard is used as an example of what not to do over a dozen times in the thirty-one chapters of Proverbs. Again, God uses the attributes of one of His creations to teach His greatest creation how to live. The truth of the matter is, this thought permeates the book of Proverbs. It is perhaps the greatest single truth that Solomon writes about. He focuses on the sluggard because the ways of the sluggard are deadly, and God wants us to live an abundant life. Just like the ant, Solomon observed the sloth and saw behaviors that could be a source of understanding how humans should behave. The difference with the sloth is Solomon discovered how *not* to live.

The sloth is a fascinating mammal, found in Central and South America. The sloth's real name is from a Hebrew word, *Atsluwth*, which means "to be idle." The sloth can literally spend its entire life in a single tree! It is the slowest of all mammals and sleeps 15 hours or more per day. Its primary occupation is eating. The sloth is so lazy, it doesn't even defend itself from predators. It just hides. Over the centuries, that hiding hasn't done a great job of protecting the sloth. In the last few centuries, nearly a dozen species of sloth have gradually become extinct, with only two common species alive today.[2]

One of my favorite passages is Proverbs 26:13-16 (NKJV). It's a great explanation of how laziness breeds fear and a reminder that we are called to be diligent and brave:

"The lazy man says, 'There is a lion in the road! A fierce lion is in the streets! As a door turns on its hinges, so does the lazy man on his bed. The lazy man buries his hand in the bowl; it wearies him to bring it back to his mouth. The lazy man is wiser in his own eyes than seven men who can answer sensibly."

Though I've experienced periods of diligence, I've also experienced periods of slothfulness, where I was lazy and reluctant and fearful. I missed out on a potential harvest because I behaved like the sloth. I accepted my circumstances instead of overcoming difficulty with faith and courage.

Thank God, more often than not, I chose to copy the ant instead of the sloth. I believe it's possible for everyone to do the same.

This book is intended to make clear the need and opportunity for all of us to be more like the ant and less like the sloth.

Throughout this book you will be presented with a challenge. It's a question that you will be asked every day as you decide how to live and how to lead yourself. The question is as follows:

Ant or Sloth?
Which one will you be?

THE MIND OF THE SLOTH

To understand any creature, it is foundational to understand how the animal thinks. Whether it's hunting and fishing, which I enjoy very much, or spider removal, which I don't, understanding the psyche and motivation of the creature is important for successfully catching or eliminating it.

The importance of understanding the mind of the sloth is simple – it's to avoid being a sloth. The actual animal that crawls slowly through treetops and eats leaves and sleeps most of the day is focused only on itself. It may live with a group of other sloths, but it is disconnected from true community by its isolation. It will remain on a single branch for days at a time. It slowly finds nourishment from the leaves around it and rarely considers that dozens, even hundreds of other living beings pass by it every day.

Much like the sloth in the trees, the slothful man is focused only on himself, to his detriment. In the New Testament, James writes a very helpful passage on this issue:

But be doers of the word, and not hearers only, deceiving yourselves. For if anyone is a hearer of the word and not a doer, he is like a man observing his natural face in a mirror; for he observes himself, goes away, and immediately forgets what kind of man he was.[3]

We are called to be doers, not just hearers. Slothfulness is an enemy, because it prevents us from being doers. The slothful man can be in the same environment as the productive man, but as the verse points out, he makes some very critical mistakes. He hears God's word but walks away. He does not diligently examine his life but rather he "forgets what manner of man he was" and is self-deceived.

THE SLOTH IS SELF-DECEIVED.

When a person follows the pattern of the sloth by living in isolation, self-deception is natural and easy to embrace. The missing feedback from others who can see your blind spots makes mistakes more likely, and eventually brings about catastrophic consequences.

Proverbs 18:1-2 (NIV) explains it very well:

A man who isolates himself seeks his own desire; he rages against all wise judgment. A fool has no delight in understanding, but in expressing his own heart.

When we live like the sloth, separated from others by either time or space, we begin to turn our attention inward. The lack of an objective person's perspective leads to the life of the fool, who doesn't care about finding out the truth, only in expressing what he or she thinks is right.

After a while, even if people who have a relationship with the isolated try to give advice, they are dismissed. They are ignored because the voice in the slothful person's head has reached a volume that drowns out everything else. If someone challenges the slothful person, they are likely to have the conversation turned back on them for suggesting something other than what the slothful fool desires.

The slothful person blames everyone or everything else instead of taking personal responsibility. Like the sloth in the tree, he waits for leaves to appear, rather than moving to an area where there is better food.

The sloth can literally starve to death instead of mustering up the courage and energy to go explore for food to live.

The slothful person is deceived but is also deceitful.

It's one thing to be deceived, but it's another level to become deceitful. The slothful person doesn't realize it at first, but slowly he or she becomes deceitful. For example, just like the sloth lives in the tree and allows algae to grow on it until it blends in with the tree, the slothful person "blends" in at the office or jobsite.

They hide in the shadows, deceiving others by looking busy without really accomplishing much. They have papers on their desk or are always talking about a project they are working on, when the reality is they might have a big checklist, but nothing ever gets checked off the list!

Most of us would deny or resist the title "lazy" if it were applied to our lives by others. The truth is, when someone is deceived, and they live in deception like the sloth, they don't notice that they are lazy. The consequence of the deception is that it overtakes the slothful person's mind and before long they find reasons to defend their laziness rather than working to come out of the life of slothfulness.

One of the greatest downsides to the isolated, self-deceived life is the diet that goes along with that kind of life. Since the sloth remains limited in its travel, it is limited in its food selection. In fact, the sloth's diet consists mostly of leaves, which have very little nutrition. The lack of nutrition leads to a lack of energy. It's a vicious cycle: the leaves give them little energy, so they stay still to conserve what strength they have. By staying still, they restrict their dietary options. As a result, the sloth's metabolism operates very slowly, which further accents the sluggish behavior.[4]

Just like the sloth's limited diet of minimal nutritional value, the self-deceived isolated person eats a diet of negativity and fear. Their diet is not one of meats and vegetables, or fruits and nuts. It's the diet of their conversation. It's the diet of their thoughts.

Jesus gave a great illustration about the power of what we say in Matthew 15:10-11 (NIV). He explained to the crowd, and offended the Pharisees when He told them all that it's not about the food we eat. It's about the things we say.

"Jesus called the crowd to Him and said, 'Listen and understand. What goes into someone's mouth does not defile them, but what comes out of their mouth, that is what defiles them'."

Over time, that diet creates a downward spiral for the self-deceived mind. The lack of faith and accountability is like the lack of nutritional value in the leaves the sloth eats. The lack of energy produced by the leaves limits the sloth's range of movement. It creates a restrictive environment.

In the same way, the lack of faith and accountability for the isolated person leads to further isolation and an increasingly restricted environment. They live in fear and live with an unwillingness to pursue anything that requires moving beyond the status quo.

So they remain, like the sloth, in an isolated, limited environment. Fear reinforces slothfulness and slothful people always listen to fearful words. In the end, the self-deception builds, the isolation compounds, and the slothful man finds himself dead to

all that God had in store for his life. Just
as the sloth, which now only has two
species remaining, with at least ten
species extinct; the slothful man ends up
extinct.

SEVEN SYMPTOMS OF THE SLOTHFUL

No one wants to end up extinct, of course. Sometimes, even the most diligent person can be slothful and not be aware of their poor choices or habits. If you're anything like me, which means you're very literal, it helps to have some clear explanation of what it looks like to be slothful. The philosophical stuff can sometimes be lacking in providing a way to actually improve.

Maybe you think you're ok. You're working hard and staying focused on your future. Remember, **no one is immune to the disease of slothfulness.** The question is how quickly do you recognize it, and how quickly do you treat it? No one wakes up and says, "Today I want to be lazy." Well, no one except for Jimmy Buffett and

Bruno Mars, who actually wrote a song called:

The Lazy Song

Bruno's song begins, "Today I don't feel like doing anything. I just want to lay in my bed!"

Now, if you're on vacation that might be okay for a little while. But, as Bruno's song indicates, everyone has a propensity or a desire to take the easy way out. If slothfulness didn't happen to everyone, he never would have written the song. But it does, and we need to be focused on it and its consequences. Don't pretend that you're immune. You're not. Everyone can be slothful. Because of this, it's important that you continually review the habits of the ant, and remember the warnings of this book. For your benefit and mine, I've included the following Seven Symptoms of the Slothful. These are valuable indicators. Avoid these at all costs!

Symptom #1:
HE DOESN'T BELIEVE HE'S SLOTHFUL

This symptom is tough to identify. But, in keeping with the pages above, the first symptom of the slothful person is deception. The only way out of the deception is to find people you respect who are straight shooters. Ask them directly if there are areas in your life that are marked by slothfulness. Don't be afraid to hear their answers. You see, the slothful behaviors are a by-product of choices to take it easy in the little things. No one has a goal to be slothful.

Since it's not a goal, it's often overlooked. When it happens, it happens in subtle ways that are easy to hide. Ask your leaders and good friends to help you examine your actions. If they identify slothfulness, be diligent to root it out and replace it with industry and determination. Go back to your family, your job, and your community with a refreshed commitment to excel.

Symptom #2:
THE SLOTHFUL ALWAYS MAKES EXCUSES

This symptom is a recurring one. It might disappear temporarily, if the slothful person has a supervisor watching them, or if they're feeling really inspired. But, the moment a challenge arises, or an obstacle appears that makes it difficult to keep going, they stop. This symptom manifests itself in the person who always has a grand ambition, but then they explain that it won't happen because of all the forces conspiring against them.

Proverbs 26:16 (NIV) reads, "A sluggard is wiser in his own eyes than seven people who answer discreetly."

The slothful person has reasons for his or her failure that make sense to them. In reality, the only area in which they aren't slothful is the area of creative excuse-making!

Don't allow yourself to make excuses. Yes, there will be obstacles to achievement. Yes, there will be bad things that happen that nobody could predict. Yes, there will be times when it seems like nothing is going right. But, that doesn't stop the ant. He just keeps chugging. Do the same.
Don't be slothful.

Don't make excuses.

Symptom #3:
THE SLOTHFUL MAKES LITTLE SOFT CHOICES

This symptom is one of the most widespread of them all. In fact, the failure of each of us to value the power of little details and small choices is probably the biggest cause of defeat in life. The Bible has a lot to say about making what I call "soft choices".

One of my favorite passages is found in Proverbs 6. It reads, *"How long will you lie there, you sluggard? When will you get up from your sleep? A little sleep, a little slumber, a little folding of the hands to rest – and poverty will come on you like a thief and scarcity like an armed man."*[5]

It doesn't take a lot for poverty to come upon us. The passage says it's just a little sleep. It's just a little slumber. It can't hurt, right? Wrong. The soft choices, the easy way leads to ruin.

It only takes hitting the snooze button a few times, until it's a habit and before long, before we know it, we are living a lazy life with scarce resources and little blessing.

Another excellent example of avoiding the "soft choices" is found in Song of Solomon 2:15. This verse is part of a passage that contains a romantic exchange between a husband and his wife. The verse encourages her to "catch…the little foxes that ruin the vineyards."[6]

In the garden, little foxes can break in and chew away at the root of the plant, and ruin all the wonderful fruit that would have been produced. In this case, it's the relationship not being tended to that leads to decay. In your own life, there are many areas that must be guarded. Don't allow the little foxes to slip in and chew away at your future harvest. Watch and work to remove them before they uproot all that is growing in your life.

Beyond the example of the little foxes, there are real examples in God's word of men and women who made the tough choices and didn't become slothful. One of the best is Joseph, the man who had big dreams. So big, his brothers nearly killed him. But no matter what happened, Joseph kept his cool and worked hard. We need to have the spirit of Joseph.

What a great example! At every stage of Joseph's life, from his brothers selling him into slavery, to his master imprisoning him on false charges, to his opportunity to stand before Pharoah, he lived with a dedication to following through on the small details.

He was so exceptional in his work ethic, even as a slave and as a prisoner, he was promoted to the highest level.[7] He made the tough choices to do all things with excellence. As a result of not compromising and not making the soft choice, he avoided slothful behavior and eventually was made second in command of the entire Egyptian empire!

Symptom #4:
THE SLOTHFUL PERSON LIVES IN A WORLD OF WISHFUL THINKING

The sluggard's basic philosophy in life is to live in the moment and let the future take care of itself. The tyranny of the immediate becomes master of his fate. These people can sometimes start well, but they end poorly. They are typically all about quick results or fast ways to make money. Of course, these schemes never last.

Remember, weeds grow quicker than trees, but at the end of the day, trees dominate.

The slothful person has lots of bright ideas, but very little initiative. They continually wish for opportunities but are unwilling to work for them. His wishes are destructive because they end up being about his sensual desires, rather than fulfilling the purposes of God.

You don't want to be a wishful thinking slothful person. No one does. But it's easy; it creeps up on you. It happens one wish at a time, one selfish thought at a time. Before long, you're lost in a world of make-believe ideas. Before long, the more unrealistic your imagination, the more likely you are to believe it. It's a steady slide away from the realities of life and diligence into a fantasy world of schemes that never pan out.

Proverbs 21:25-26 (NKJV) reads, *"The desire of the lazy man kills him, for his hands refuse to labor. He covets greedily all day long, but the righteous gives and does not spare."*

It's not known if the sloth in its natural habitat is lost in wishful thinking. It's not known if the sloth has the level of intellect necessary to have thoughts beyond a very basic level. However, sloths do not exhibit a very limited activity level, which would confirm their unwillingness to act on thoughts of ambition, if they did have any.

We do know that sloths sleep. A lot. Sloths in captivity sleep anywhere from 15 to 20 hours a day.[8] Could it be that the lack of anything motivational in its environment leads to a life of slumber?

Proverbs 26:14 (NIV) reads, *"As a door turns on its hinges, so a sluggard turns on his bed."* It's that easy. Like a swinging door, the slothful person returns to sleep. He might be momentarily awakened to an opportunity but he quickly defeats it before even giving it a chance. He closes his eyes and returns to the land of dreams. He breathes a sigh and enters the fantasy world of his imagination. He pulls the blankets up tight and resumes his life of wishful thinking.

If you find yourself around people who spend their days in wishful thinking, or if you are prone to do the same, this is your opportunity to change. Shake off the sneaky sleep that takes away your life and leads to extinction. Avoid conversations that place blame and aren't constructive. Choose to live. Choose to follow the example of the ant. If you feel insignificant or under-prepared, read on. Look to one of the smallest yet strongest creatures that God has created for inspiration.

To avoid this symptom of slothfulness, surround yourself with experienced, successful counsel. Share your ideas with them, and if they tell you that you're being unrealistic, listen. Anyone can dream, not everyone can do. Find the doers. Follow the doers. **Become a doer and avoid the slothful symptom of wishful thinking.**

Symptom #5:
THE SLOTHFUL PERSON BRINGS NEGATIVE MOMENTUM TO THEIR ENVIRONMENT

I often say it's better to pay a slothful person to stay home from work than to have them at work! Their very presence is actually worse than their absence. How can this be? It's simple, really.

They carry a negative character that can infect the diligent people around them. It becomes costly for your business and your relationships when you have to count on a slothful person.

They miss deadlines.
They turn in incomplete work.

They show up late and leave early. They rarely finish what they start.

These are just a few examples, but I think you get the point. Proverbs 18:9 (NIV) reads, *"One who is slack in his work is brother to one who destroys."*

You see, being slothful is just as bad as being outright destructive. Actually, I think it might be worse. At least with the destructive person, you know they are out to cause damage and wreak havoc. With the slothful person, they look like they are on your side, but slowly and surely, they are chipping away at everything around them, bringing everything they touch to ruin.

The negativity they bring is more than an emotion. It's a negative momentum that prevents growth and limits potential.

In work and family relationships, the slothful person's failure to fulfill his or her obligations creates problem for everyone. They procrastinate. They delay. Over time, they become, "as vinegar to the teeth and smoke to the eyes."[9] That's not a nice description. Imagine if your presence caused people to feel like they were drinking vinegar or coughing through smoke-filled eyes!

That's what happens to the environment when a slothful person enters. The person who fails to be diligent leaves a mess for others to clean.

One of the most embarrassing moments in my life happened because I was slothful. And my slothfulness put a good friend in a bad position, and negatively affected dozens of people.

I share this story in my book, *The Accent of Leadership: Words Matter.* I'll keep it brief but it's good to repeat here. It makes the point very well, unfortunately, at my expense.

Years ago, I was in charge of Hillsong Bible College. I had a guest speaker, who was also a friend, in town to speak to the entire student body. This was a great opportunity for the students to hear an inspiring message. In the weeks and months leading up to his visit, I would pass by our guest room (where he ended up staying) and notice that the bathroom doorknob was loose.

"I need to fix that," I'd tell myself. As you've probably guessed, I put it off and never fixed the doorknob. On the morning my friend was scheduled to speak, I had already left for work. He was getting ready in that same bathroom.

After showering, he pulled on the doorknob to go into the attached bedroom, and the entire knob came off in his hand! He was stuck inside the bathroom!

Meanwhile, I was trying to call him, as an auditorium full of students was waiting for him to speak. He remained locked in my guest room bath because I failed to fix the problem. My slothfulness brought negative momentum to that day for everyone!

Employers, be wise in your hiring. Employees, be wise in your relationships at work. Associate with everyone, but collaborate with the diligent. Choose to avoid the area that the slothful inhabit. Refuse to be ruled by lack. Expand your vision, stay disciplined, and you will find the abundant provision you need to live with excellence – in every area of your life.

Check the little things in your life, your work, and your relationships. Maybe you started an exercise regimen and abandoned it. Maybe you have a project you keep procrastinating. Whatever it is, avoid being slothful. Be like the ant. Bring positive momentum to your environment!

Symptom #6:
THE SLOTHFUL IS A VICTIM OF SELF-INDUCED FEARS

The greatest fuel for slothfulness is fear. Fear reinforces the most natural response of the sloth, which is withdrawal. Rather than face its problems, the sloth hides. Rather than fight for the best, rather than work for excellence, the slothful person points out the dangers in the world, real or imagined. "The sluggard says, 'There is a lion in the road, a fierce lion roaming the streets!"[10]

Have you ever noticed how some people respond to new ideas by pointing out the threats that might prevent them from succeeding? These are slothful people. They are bound by fear, and they spread the seeds of fear by focusing on the potential danger that exists everywhere. But, the truth is, every day is filled with danger, if you choose to see it that way.

I prefer to see the opportunity. Every day is loaded with potential! Only the slothful person refuses to see how much good is before us. Only the slothful person finds reasons to run and hide.

I've heard the following acronym many times, and perhaps you have as well. It's a very accurate description of fear:

False
Evidence
Appearing
Real

If perception is reality, it's clear that the slothful person has chosen to accept the false evidence of danger as a substitute for the faithful excellence of God's provision. It's a shame. So much is lost because of self-induced fears. So much hope is lost. So much joy is lost. So much blessing is lost.

All because of the willingness to embrace fear and avoid faith.

Don't be slothful. Don't buy into the lies of FEAR. The next time you begin to talk about how hard things are, or how dangerous the world is, remember that God is bigger than any problem. God is greater than any danger. He is "able to do exceedingly abundantly above all that we ask or think."[11]

God doesn't have any problem with our big dreams. He is able to provide, provided we do our part. If you have a problem with fear, ask for help. Arrest your thoughts, and renew your mind. Pick up a copy of Choose: Your Daily Decisions Determine Your Destiny. It will give you the basics you need to renew your world and refuse fear. Turn off the negative news shows. Listen to positive worship. Read God's promises. Trust Him and be diligent. You will see the potential you once thought long gone resurface in your life.

43

Symptom #7:
THE SLOTHFUL VIEWPOINT IS UPSIDE DOWN

The sloth spends most of its time upside down, hanging in a tree. It rarely sees the ground. Its vision is focused on the leaves around it and the slivers of sunlight that peek through the foliage.

Much like the sloth in the tree, the slothful person's perspective is upside-down. It's not grounded. It's a pie-in-the-sky mindset that prevents them from seeing reality. For example, the slothful person sees achievement as simply an increase in work. Even maintaining what he has is a burden for the slothful man.

Ecclesiastes 10:18 (WEB) states, "By slothfulness the roof sinks in; and through idleness of the hands the house leaks."

Whether through procrastination, which is simply scheduled laziness, or through distraction, the self-deceived slothful man persists in avoiding reality.

The sloth that hangs in the trees in South America doesn't make any sudden movements for two reasons. First, its metabolism is the slowest of any mammal. Second, its lack of movement is a defense mechanism.[12]

Some of us may be inclined to think that stationary hiding is an effective defense against predators. Remaining motionless is the way the sloth tries to avoid attack.

Unfortunately, the harpy eagle, a predatory bird that enjoys devouring sloths, has no inhibitions regarding attacking the sloth. Its keen eyesight enables it to see through the branches, and its rapid descent, talons poised to snatch, allow the harpy eagle to swoop down and grab a nice meal without thinking twice.

As Dr. Donald Moore of the National Zoo in Washington, DC, says, "There's no real defense against something that's willing to dive bomb a tree, flip upside down and grab you off a vine."[13]

The lesson for us is that a lack of activity is never a defense from those who would like to take us out. As the sloth considers its options and chooses to hide, if we allow threats to keep us from moving, we not only can't defeat the threats, we become sitting ducks! The sloth's lack of awareness and vision prevent it from considering the alternatives that may lead to safety and life. Part of the problem is its life is spent mostly upside down.

No wonder it fails to appreciate the reality of the world it lives in.

When we live like the sloth, our view of the world is skewed. We don't see things right side up, like God desires. When we fix our eyes on Him, and especially His Word, we find the truth for our lives and the vision for our road ahead. Most Christians are familiar with the following verse from Hebrews 4 – "For the word of God is living and active and sharper than any two-edged sword, and piercing as far as the division of soul and spirit of both joints and marrow, and able to judge the thoughts and intentions of the heart."[14]

God's word gives us the truth. It clarifies our purpose and gives our eyes the ability to see what's right. It's notable that the verse right after the one above reads, "And there is no creature hidden from His sight, but all things are open and laid bare to the eyes of Him with whom we have to do."[15]

The sloth has a limited, upside down view. God does not. God has a vision that sees every creature, and nothing is hidden from Him. His Word judges the thoughts and intentions of our hearts and cuts to the truth. Focus on His Word and dedicate yourself to seeing with the eyes of God. The eyes of faith will set your course, and will propel you into a life much more abundant, much more prominent, and most of all, much more fulfilled, than could ever possibly be had by only looking at limited scenery from a distorted perspective.

CONQUER
SLOTHFULNESS

I just spent a good part of this book sharing symptoms of slothfulness. Maybe you saw yourself in one of them. Or more than one. I know, at some point in my life, I've seen myself in all of them. Remember, no one is immune from slothfulness. The great news is no one has to remain slothful. This chapter contains some powerful ways to conquer slothfulness. Review them and apply them. Be consistent. Remember, neither the ant nor the sloth creates their world in a single day.

Likewise, we must repeatedly apply the principles below to fully conquer slothfulness and become the productive leader God wants us to be.

STAY HUNGRY

It might seem a little strange to say hunger is a way to conquer slothfulness. Stay with me. One of the most well-known scriptures is found in 2 Thessalonians 3:10 (NIV): *"For even when we were with you, we gave you this rule:* ***The one who is unwilling to work shall not eat."***

Paul wrote this in his letter to the church at Thessalonica. He was guiding them in how to manage the community that had sprung up around the church. A couple verses earlier, he said (of himself and his team) ***"nor did we eat anyone's food without paying for it.*** On the contrary, we worked night and day, laboring and toiling so that we would not be aburden to any of you."[16]

This is an interesting and important teaching. In the early church, we are often told, people shared and those who had gave to those who didn't. While that's true, nowhere does Paul say to be idle and just take a free handout. I've heard people argue for welfare benefits and other government subsidies based on the notion that the early church was a socialist environment. It was a true community, but Paul's strong teaching in his letter to the Thessalonians confirms the reality that God desires that we work.

Thus, my point. Hunger cures slothfulness because hunger is a good motivator for us to work. One of the ways I break a lazy spell in my own life is through fasting. Hunger is not a bad thing. It's a powerful force, and it can be channeled for great focus and work.

Don't get me wrong. I'm all for helping the poor. But, we shouldn't give freely to able-bodied people who are able to work. I heard a friend say it best, "we should do enough to help the poor stay alive but not enough for them to sit around comfortably."

Maybe that sounds harsh to you. But, it's harsher in the long run to allow capable people to thwart their potential by living on handouts. Maybe it's the opposite in your case. Maybe you're blessed beyond measure. Maybe you haven't been hungry in years or decades. Over time, you've allowed slothfulness to creep in because you haven't known desperation in a long time.

The Rocky movie series, starring Sylvester Stallone, provide a great illustration of this truth. In *Rocky III*, he had won the title. He was on top of the world, and he was "living the dream".

Along came "Clubber Lang", played by Mr. T. They were set up for a boxing match, and Rocky got beat soundly. Because he was the champion, and he hadn't been hungry in a while, Rocky took the bout for granted and was pummeled by the challenger.

Hunger is a powerful force against slothfulness, whether you're at the top or you're at the bottom in life. If you've gotten comfortable, make a decision to get hungry again. Find a way to eliminate the things in your life that are keeping you soft. Push through the ease of modern life and get hungry for greater things.

BE DILIGENT

There's a reason Proverbs repeatedly encourages us to "Go to the Ant". The ant is the embodiment of diligence. It finishes what it starts and it respects the seasons of life. It is relentless. It pursues its goals regardless of interruption or obstacle. That's why Proverbs tells us to "Go to the Ant".

Proverbs doesn't tell us to "Go to the Grasshopper". Now, I'm not sure that grasshoppers are lazy or diligent, but there's often truth in ancient stories, and one of the oldest of all is the story of the Ant and the Grasshopper, to which we now turn to consider the importance of diligence in conquering slothfulness.

Do you remember the old story about the Ant and the Grasshopper[17]? Perhaps you may recall it from your childhood. Attributed to Aesop, the story has been told for centuries. Its timeless moral provides a vivid reminder of the importance of anticipating every season in life, and preparing for the future, even when things are going great. Especially when things are going great!

Though the book you're reading is about the differences between the ant and the sloth, I couldn't pass up throwing in another creature. The grasshopper in Aesop's fable is a perfect illustration of the foolishness of procrastination. While the grasshopper spends the sunny days of summer singing and dancing, the ants work to store up food for the winter. The grasshopper mocks and ridicules the ants. He begs them to come have fun, to enjoy the warm weather. He tells them that there will be plenty of time to work.

Fast forward a few months, as the story goes, and the grasshopper has nothing to eat. An early winter storm has blown in, and snow blankets the ground. The shivering grasshopper begs to be given food but he can find no comfort. The ants have locked themselves away, warm and well-fed. They are comfortable and calm because they anticipated the weather to come.

The ant is like the Boy Scout of the insect world. Always prepared! Because of its physiology, it works the most when the weather is warm. Like many animals and bugs, the ant's energy and activity is affected by temperature.

As the nest cools in the fall, ants become weaker and are unable to work. Not only do they plan for the external seasons, they are also prepared for their own limitations.

There's a valuable lesson for us in the diligence of the ant. It anticipates what is coming, and stays focused on the task at hand. It's much more common for us to think about the external changes and challenges that might affect our lives. But, how often do we consider our internal weaknesses – like the ant's inability to work in the cold? The ant, of course, behaves in a self-preserving way because of instinct. The Christian, however, has something even better than instinct inside of him or her. We have the voice of God, through His Holy Spirit. We just have to listen.

The guide for our life that was sent by God when Jesus left Earth, the Holy Spirit is available and desires to help us anticipate the areas of life that require our attention and energy. If we listen to Him, we will be protected and prepared for the temptations around the corner.

Seek His voice. Listen to His promptings. He will guide you and prepare you for the coming winter seasons.

Stay steady, stay focused. Work with a long-term vision. Remember the grasshopper, but even more, remember the ant. Be diligent.

If you're currently unemployed, treat your job search like it's your job. Get up at 9 am and search for jobs all day. Send out resumes, fill out applications. Take a coffee break mid-morning. Take a forty-five minute lunch. Don't stop looking for work until 5 pm. The next day, repeat the cycle, until you get a job. I guarantee, if you follow this advice, you won't be unemployed long. You may have to take a job you don't necessarily want, but take it. Your diligence will pay off, you'll find promotion and opportunity that will amaze you. Be diligent. Be like the ant.

WAKE UP EARLY

"Early to bed, and early to rise, makes a man healthy, wealthy, and wise." So the old saying, attributed to Ben Franklin, goes. Everyone's heard it, but not everyone does it. In fact, on the occasion that our early Sunday service seems a little tired, I ask everyone to raise their hands if they are a "morning" person. I would say that it's less than 1/4 of the crowd, if that, who like to wake up early.

Again, we are fighting the flesh. The slothful nature in our bodies wants to sleep. The warm blankets and the comfortable bed feels so much better than the sound of the screeching alarm, jarring us awake. It's easy to slip back into slumber. That's how it happens. Easily. We give into our slothfulness and before long, we've created a habit of sleeping more than necessary.

I told you I was going to be practical. It's hard to get more practical than this point – **Wake Up Early!**

This isn't something I came up with on my own. This isn't something that's only for the military or Olympic athletes. This is for everyone. God says, "those who seek me early and diligently will find Me…"[18] Not only will rising early allow you to "find" God before the noise and bustle of the day, it will also give you a head start on your day ahead. It provides you with clarity and focus so you start off from a place of stability, instead of a place of delay. Don't take my word for it, here's a few verses from God that make it clear how important it is to wake up early:

"Do not love sleep or you will grow poor. Stay awake and you will have food to spare." – *Proverbs 20:13 (NIV)*

*"He who gathers crops in summer is a prudent son, but **he who sleeps during harvest is a disgraceful son.**"* – Proverbs 10:5 (NIV)

"Laziness casts into a deep sleep, and an idle man will suffer hunger." – Proverbs 19:15 (NASB)

God is actually more concerned with us sleeping too much than not enough. In fact, the Bible is filled with examples of people who slept too much and failed to do what God wanted, and it's filled with people who rose early and did great things for God as a result. I like to call this the "Sleep Test". Basically, the test is this: do you love sleep? Do you look for opportunities to "sleep in"? Or do you rise early, seeking God, and pursuing greatness?

Let's look at the following examples of those in the Bible who failed and those who passed the Sleep Test. Below is a little quiz; don't worry, all the answers are provided. As you read through them, try to guess who the person might be. You might be surprised when you see the answers!

1. God asked me to anoint the new ruler of the nation of Israel. I got up early in the morning in order to carry out His instructions. Who am I?

2. I was startled by the words, "O sleeper, get up and call on your God." This was a rebuke to me and it revealed my slothfulness, which was a by-product of my rebellious spirit. Who am I?

3. God asked me to perform a very difficult task – surrendering my most cherished affection. I got up early in the morning to carry out His assignment. Who am I?

4. I had a habit of falling asleep when I should have been running from temptation. My enjoyment of inappropriate sleep cost me my spiritual and physical vision. Who am I?

5. I needed direction from God for a major decision. I asked God to work out certain circumstances and I got up early in the morning to find His answer. Who am I?

6. A slothful person does not anticipate future needs, and that was my problem. Because of it, I lost the opportunity of a lifetime. Who am I?

7. I got up a great while before daylight so I could have time alone in prayer with my heavenly Father. Who am I?

What an interesting group of people. Each one of them was either used by God in part because they rose early, or failed in God's assignment because they loved sleep! Think you know who they are? Turn the page to find out!

1. The prophet **Samuel** was called by
    God to anoint David as the next king
    of Israel. He rose early and obeyed
    God.(1 Samuel 9:26)

2. The prophet **Jonah** was punished for
    his slothful rebellion by getting thrown
    into the ocean and swallowed by a
    whale. (Jonah 1:6)

3. **Abraham** was commanded by god to
    sacrifice his son. Rather than hiding in
    sleep, he rose early. God honored his
    heart and spared his son. (Genesis 22:3)

4. **Samson** might be the ultimate in
    slothfulness. Though he was physically
    strong, he was weak in his spirit and he
    gave into his desires to sleep, costing
    him everything. (Judges 16:19)

5. **Gideon** wanted assurances from God that he really was called to lead the Israelites out of captivity. He awoke early to discover that God was with him and he obeyed God, leading Israel to a miraculous victory. (Judges 6:38)

6. **The Foolish Virgin** wasn't prepared for the bridegroom to come, and was left out of the wedding because she had no oil in her lamp. Her slothful lack of preparation cost her a once-in-a-lifetime opportunity. (Matthew 25:5)

7. **Jesus** sought time early in the morning to talk with God. He knew that every day mattered, and so He started each day with what mattered most: hearing from God. (Mark 1:35)

RESPECT TIME

You can't save time. You can only spend
it. While that may be a cliché, the truth is
expressions become cliché because they
are true. When it comes to time, there is a
limited amount available to each person,
and it's up to us to make the most of our
days.

We only have a brief window of
productivity on this earth, and if we don't
respect time, we will turn around after a
lifetime and be filled with regret for the
things we failed to accomplish. Here's a
sobering passage from the book of Psalms:

*You (God) turn people back to dust, saying,
"Return to dust, you mortals." A thousand years
in your sight are like a day that has just gone by,
or like a watch in the night. Yet you sweep people
away in the sleep of death – they are like the new
grass of the morning: In the morning it springs up
new, but by evening it is dry and withered.*[19]

Just like that, our life has come and gone. Like a blade of grass that appears in the morning and is withered in a day, we spring up, have our day in the sun, and move on to heaven.

I'm not trying to be morbid. I'm not trying to depress you. I'm trying to motivate you. Understand that time is precious – the most precious commodity we have. Just like in the story of the Grasshopper and the Ant, we must look to the ant and redeem every day that we have. Be accountable to yourself, your calendar, and allow others to hold you accountable for idle actions, and wasted days.

Respecting time is not just something we do for ourselves. Even more important is respecting other people's time. I have often been in meetings where a person shows up five minutes late. Usually, everyone extends them grace, but if it becomes a habit, it's a red flag to me that they don't respect other people's time.

Think about it, if you are five minutes late for a meeting with ten other people, you have wasted only five minutes of your time, **but you've wasted a collective 50 minutes of everyone else's time. That's nearly an hour lost because you didn't respect other people's time.**

Life goes fast. As I write this I'm about to become a grandfather. Like many people, I now find myself saying, "It seems like only yesterday, I was just getting married...".

There is no substitute for time. There is no time bank that we can make withdrawals from when we run low. There is only the days you've – and I've – been given. Make the very most of them. Set your schedule and follow it. Be punctual. Be early. Follow through with your appointments. Respect other people's time. Remember, today is all you're guaranteed. Like the ant, make the most of it!

GO TO THE ANT

Of all the animals that God tells us to look to for inspiration and an example, it's not the bold lion, it's not the strong ox. It's not the proud eagle, nor is it the super swift cheetah. God sends us to the ant. Maybe it's because He wants us to understand it doesn't take special abilities to follow His plan. It just takes consistent application of His truth and it requires collaboration with the many great people in our lives.

STRENGTH

I suppose the ant does have one "super power". But even that power, its strength, is only effective when done in collaboration with others. It's an understatement to say that the ant is strong.

As science has developed and studied nature over the past few centuries, many remarkable facts have been uncovered about the anatomy of the ant. In particular, the ant has a tremendous amount of strength relative to its size.

Based on size to strength ratios, if the ant were a human, it would be Superman. A leaf-cutter ant can carry up to 20 times its own weight over a 100 meters – that's the equivalent to a 200-pound man carrying 2 tons on his back for 17 miles![20]

In a single day, the ant may take as many as four round trips as far away as 400 feet from its home. Extrapolating that out to the human dimension, that would be roughly the equivalent of a man walking 68 miles. If the ant had the stride of a man, it could have bursts of speed up to 65 miles an hour.

There is a species of ant, the driver ant, that can literally take down an ox when working in collaboration with its fellow ants. They migrate in long columns, eating every piece of flesh in their path. Reports have been made of caged leopards being reduced to bones overnight by a swarm of driver ants. There was even a report of an elephant that could escape and was completely consumed in three days!

Collectively, ants rival human beings as the most dominant organism on land. Their sheer volume and interconnected strength leads them to have great power as they roam across planet earth.[21]

The feats of the ant are indeed extraordinary. One of the most impressive aspects of the ant's strength is its collective heft to get big jobs done. The ant reminds me of an expression that we use all the time in Wave Church. When we face significant challenges, we compare it to "eating an elephant".

Do you know how to eat an elephant? You don't get overwhelmed, you don't get intimidated. You roll up your sleeves, and take it "one bite at a time". When we work together, like the ant, anything is possible. The individual and collective strength of the ant is a tremendous example to all of us.

DETERMINATION

What does it take to slow you down? What does it take to stop you? Physical strength is only one attribute of the ant.

Its body is equipped to move mountains, but the greatest body in the world alone is insufficient to accomplish great feats. More than just strength is required. The strength of will is necessary to move forward. Sometimes you just have to keep going, even when you're overwhelmed, or at a disadvantage.

In my book, *The Accent of Leadership: Words Matter,* I share the true story of Steven Bradbury, an Australian speed skater who won the first Australian Winter Olympic gold medal. In case you didn't know, Australia isn't known for its winter sports! How did Steven Bradbury win? Was he extra talented? No. Was he super fast? No. He was simply determined. In the final race of the 2002 Winter Olympics in Salt Lake City, Utah, as the racers came around the final curve into the home stretch, a series of trips and mishaps led to all the skaters in front of him falling down. He cruised right through to the gold medal as the others tried to pick themselves up off the ice!

This might seem lucky or even silly, but think about it. If he hadn't entered the race because he wasn't as fast as the others, he would be sitting at home today without an Olympic gold medal. You never know what could happen to the people in front of you in life. Stay in the race!

Often, in overcoming obstacles, determination makes all the difference. So it is for the ants, who systematically and consistently do their work. So it is for us, who are called to do great work for God, and who are called to help build the local church.

Back to my question – *what does it take to stop you?*

From my perspective, persistence is a greater asset than talent. The diligent application of energy to a task will lead to the kind of results that others applaud, and most importantly, that God favors. If you find it difficult to keep going when things get boring or tedious, or overwhelming, your response should be the same. Look to the ant. It is resolved to do whatever its job may be. As a consequence of each ant staying on task, the whole community flourishes. This is a great example for us.

Many times, I've watched people fall away from a path that was taking them to success. They dropped out because someone else got a promotion they wanted. Or, they gave up because a task was "beneath" them. Whatever the reason, the absence of determination led to a poor outcome and a life of lack.

God desires abundance for us all. He desires that we observe the ant and learn from its strength and determination. But God isn't going to do everything for us. He wants us to develop our strength. He wants us to remain persistent, even when we don't feel like it. In Galatians 6:7-9, God explains how we must remain determined to receive and achieve the best for our lives:

*"Do not be deceived, God is not mocked; for whatever a man sows, that he will also reap. For he who sows to his flesh will of the flesh reap corruption, but he who sows to the Spirit will of the Spirit reap everlasting life. **And let us not grow weary while doing good, for in due season we will reap if we do not faint.**"*

You see, even if our physical strength wanes, and it likely will, our choice to remain determined makes all the difference. The choice to be persistent and to follow God's wisdom will lead to success, in whatever venture you pursue. In my book Choose: Your Daily Decisions Determine Your Destiny, I explain how the power of determination makes the difference, and I believe enables you to remain determined even in the face of difficult challenges:

"Often, success is found through simple persistence. In business, in relationships, in athletic training, in every human competition, achievement comes – almost by default – by being the last man standing. **The willingness of a person to persevere is the key attribute for any measure of achievement.**[22]

No matter what you're doing, if it's honorable and right, my encouragement remains the same. Stay persistent. Take it "one bite at a time". Like the ant, your determination will carry you through the roadblocks and lead to the successful completion and achievement that your heart – and God's – desires.

GOVERNMENT

As mentioned earlier, the ant does everything in collaboration with other ants. No ant survives in isolation. Every ant needs a leader, and that only happens in the ant's God-ordained environment, the colony. In the colony, the queen is the center of attention because she is the source of all new life, and the perpetuation of the colony. She is not, however, the chief ruler.

There are a group of older ants who are servant leaders. Their job is to do the work of building and maintaining the anthill, and in so doing, they serve as a model for the younger ants. They don't have official titles or positions, they just do the work.

It's the same in God's house, the local church. The colony of faithful believers that build the work of Jesus and bring others to Him are simply dedicated workers who don't require titles or positions. The value of what they do is matched by the humility in which they serve. And, as a result, the next generation is trained and new Christians join the colony.

One other aspect of the government of the ant is fascinating. When worker ants go in search of food outside the anthill, they actually leave a trail that contains a scent. The other ants can then follow the trail to the nutrition they need.

In your own life, what kind of trail are you blazing? Are you leaving a scent behind that brings others to life- giving and life-sustaining nutrition? I'm not talking about food, I'm talking about the love of Jesus, the grace of God, the power of the Holy Spirit. No matter what your situation, you are leading someone. Are they following you to a better place? Are they following you to health and abundant life?

The government of the ant is critical for the entire colony's survival. The order that God instituted by making the local church the fulfillment of the work of Jesus on this earth is critical for the survival of the entire human population. Work. Serve. Lead. Grow.

COMMUNITY

The ant colony is everything. Without the community life, the ant would quickly be rendered extinct. They simply aren't made to thrive without others. It's the same for you and me. We need others in our lives, and others need us.

Did you know that the ants have a built-in drive-thru "car wash" in their colony? When the worker ants return from a foraging expedition, they are greeted by young ants who lick the worker ants clean. They give special care to the antenna, which is the organ that enables the ant to sense danger and find its way home. The younger ants clean the worker ants to help keep them clean and sharp for what the next day holds.

Church is like a drive-through "car wash" for the soul. When we gather together to worship God, we are encouraged by our fellow believers. We might be dirty and dingy and dinged up from the week's work, but when we enter God's house, we get refreshed and cleaned. Our soul becomes strengthened, and our antennas become sharp – ready for what the next week holds.

EYES ON THE SUN

Finally, we can go to the ant to understand how to find our way. Life is not easy, and we consistently face challenges that threaten to knock us off course. We may not always see things clearly, but we can once again turn to the ant to understand where to look.

The ant's eyes are a cluster of tiny prisms that create a mosaic effect. It doesn't have the ability to see with any real detail. As a result, beyond 2.5 centimeters, the eye of the ant is virtually blind. It's only able to differentiate between light and dark, between sun and shadow.

Like the ant, as we peer into the future and try to see what God has for us, we can't really get a clear image. Everything is blurry and unknown. But, like the ant, we can recognize the difference between light and dark. The ants allows its ability to see light to position it on its path. Ants align with the sun to maneuver correctly through tall grass. Think about it – other than concrete, everywhere the ant walks it has some type of plant that overshadows it. But the ant's ability to detect the sun allows it to find its ways even in the jungle. They simply keep their bodies at the right angle to maintain exposure to the sun.

What a lesson for us! Even when we can't see where we are going (and most of the time we can't), we can trust God's Son. If we look to Jesus, He will guide us, just like the ant, through the jungle of life.

The ant. What a remarkable creation. The sloth. What a fascinating waste of potential. We have a choice every day to be like one or the other. My prayer is that this book has encouraged you to pursue the example of the ant. Push aside slothful behaviors and thinking. Align your mind and your actions with the strength, determination, and government of the ant. Go the extra mile. Keep your eyes on Jesus. As time passes, you'll discover a life worth living – when you live like the ant!

Don't close the book yet. You're not done!

Apply the ant's example right now. Take the slothfulness quiz on the next few pages and see how readily you recognize the difference between living like the sloth and living like the ant. Check your score on the last page. If you miss more than four questions, I recommend you review this book again. Keep it on your mind. Push aside slothfulness in yourself and others. Lead yourself and lead others. The life of the ant is waiting for you!

THE SLOTHFULNESS QUIZ

1. A slothful man is one who really does not want to get anything out of life.

True False

2. The main occupation of a sluggard is sitting around watching others do work.

True False

3. Because a slothful man skillfully gets out of work, he avoids the pressures of life.

True False

4. A slothful man will not usually work for somebody else, but he will work for himself.

True False

5. A slothful man will not work, nor will he give excuses for not working.

True False

6. A slothful man is very aware that he is slothful.

True False

7. If a slothful man is hired, he will bring his employer neither gain nor loss.

True False

8. A slothful man finds everything difficult, even eating his food.
True False

9. The slothful lives in an unrealistic world.

True False

10. One way to conquer slothfulness is to give a man the responsibility of having his own business.

True False

11. If a slothful man is to be helped at all, his food supply must be taken from him.

True False

12. God says that a diligent man is not able to learn anything from the life of a slothful man.

True False

13. For an employer to get anything out of a slothful man, he must give him continual prodding.

True False

14. A sluggard is just an ordinary person who makes little surrenders to his sensual desires.

True False

15. A sluggard is a very weak-willed person.

True False

16. The slothful mind is as sluggish as his body.

True False

17. God has no counsel for a sluggard.

True False

18. One way to help a sluggard is to show him cause and effect sequences.

True False

19. A sluggard likes to begin things but not finish them.

True False

20. A sluggard will appreciate one who prods him to work.

True False

THE SLOTHFULNESS QUIZ: ANSWERS

1. FALSE
2. FALSE
3. FALSE
4. FALSE
5. FALSE
6. FALSE
7. FALSE
8. TRUE
9. TRUE
10. FALSE
11. TRUE
12. FALSE
13. TRUE
14. TRUE
15. TRUE
16. FALSE
17. FALSE
18. FALSE
19. TRUE
20. FALSE

1. Psalm 37:4 (NKJV)
2. Gardner, A. (2005). Wilson, D. E.; Reeder, D. M, eds. Mammal Species of the World (3rd ed.). Johns Hopkins University Press. pp. 100–101.
3. James 1:22-24
4. http://slothfacts.org
5. Proverbs 6:9-11 (NIV)
6. Song of Solomon 2:15 (NIV)
7. Genesis 37-50
8. http://www.livescience.com/27612sloths.html
9. Proverbs 10:26 (NIV)
10. Proverbs 26:13 (NIV)
11. Ephesians 3:20 (NIV)
12. Moore, Donald, PhD, Associate Director of animal care, Smithsonian National Zoo, Washington, DC. Media interview
13. http://earjecosystem.weebly.com
14. Hebrews 4:12
15. Hebrews 4:13
16. 2 Thessalonians 3:8 (NIV)
17. Ben Edwin Perry (1965). Babrius and Phaedrus. Loeb Classical Library. Cambridge, MA: Harvard University Press. pp. 487, no. 373.
18. Proverbs 8:17 (AMP)
19. Psalm 90:3-6 (NIV)
20. http://lingolex.com/ants.htm
21. Wilson, Edward O., & Holldobler, Bert. Journey to the Ants: A Story of Scientific Exploration, Harvard University Press (1994)
22. Kelly, Steve, Choose: Your Daily Decisions Determine Your Destiny, page 24. Wave Publishing, LLC (2013)

Made in the USA
Columbia, SC
05 September 2021

44962599R00052